GUNPOWDER SQUARE

Gabriel Olearnik

The right of Gabriel Olearnik to be identified as author of this work has been asserted by him in accordance with the Copyright, Designs and Patents Act 1988.

This is a work of fiction. Any similarity of persons, places or events depicted here into actual persons, places or events is purely coincidental.

Copyright ©2011 by Gabriel Olearnik
All rights reserved
Published by Three Shoes Books, Cheltenham

In "Palms" the quotation in italics is from Byzantine Art by Robin Cormack (2000) and is used by permission of Oxford University Press.

ISBN 978-1-4475-1581-4

GUNPOWDER SQUARE

Gabriel Olearnik

Three Shoes Books

Contents

The Clotheshorse, the ghost of London	7
The words we write	9
The beetle and the piano	10
Hamlet, reviewed	11
First edition	12
A prayer before retiring	13
Bitterness	14
Box	15
Companion	16
Faith	17
The Wilton Diptych	18
Rood	19
Saffron	20
Professor	21
Brutus	22
Auxiliary	23
Temptation	24
Toledo	25
Stallion	27
Galliard	28
Asp	30
Canticle	31
Rossetti's changeling	32
Priestess	33
Composition	34
The summer country	35
Noon	36
Katana	37
Aphex	39
Outremer	40

Homecoming	41
Émigré	42
Hetman	43
Neva's Queen	44
The third of May	45
A Silesian coalman's return	46
Poznan	47
Horae mortis	48
Power	49
Torrent	50
The guard of flowers	51
Candlemas	52
Cog	53
The Decollation of St James	55
Palms	56
Notes	57

The Clotheshorse, the ghost of London

London wears the stories of discarded garments.
London speaks in the tear of fabric.
London — we are here. Tell the tale of the clotheshorse.

It is a stripping tale. Time must be shorn of its garments
and you, audience, dressed by thought, before you can catch
The Dart of Cloth.
That is its name: the clotheshorse, that beast of fangs, a winterdyke
and doom.
Its truth prickles like nettles on the skin.

London, begin.

Eden Club, Soho, a belt

In this music you are impudent, carved bones and pounced stares
an oriental valet, a sultan of cats.
The lip of your trouser scuttled in blue.
You quarrel with your legs. Your face bleeds from its cheeks.
The family face. Shame the first parent.

Initio, an argument of fruit - the naveless ate no apples.
They sewed aprons of fig leaves.
Conclusio, a fig screwed the human race.
Are you impressed? But feline face, you argue with your arms
my position may be amended
I leave my vitals unattended.

High Street Kensington, a baby bonnet

Wrestling the buggy, you come direct, alluring in smell

singeing, intrusive, like the aroma of some exotic weed
ablaze, shuddering, the strings of a voice
creeping through the crevices of the crowd
high on the palate like aromatic bitters
resounding, rebounding, infecting
the unpolluted scurry of my mouth.

Seven years and there you are.
(The bonnet falls unnoticed).

Vietnamese café, Old Street, a beret

Barely blind, bespectacled, sniffing the cloth of a novel.
Truffle-deep in thought,
a humus-humour, I being my own distraction.
The lives of others, the thoughts of others
at one remove, like a relative of forty years mutuality
not talking, but a nod impermanently exchanged.
It would be unfair to tire them with speech.
Everything wriggling and dull has been exposed.
And whilst I burrow into the soft soil of my own mood,
an unknown hand reaches over and takes my beret.

The words we write

Sophia — I stripped myself bare this morning
bare of words like shrouds
(the dawn kissing my neck's nape, not you)
and attended the moment: the arguments of schools.

I

The first ghost hissed its rage
its tongue aflame with words of fire
and a voice like burned sugar:

"Perfection. The common clay will harden in the heat. Words
are sweet, brilliant, fleet. Homme lubrique, crémé au lait.
For us immortals, crémé brûlée."

II

The second spectre answered slow, with wet words, gargled, low:

"Plain. Write of universal joy and simple pain.
Open words, digestable and sane.
The mother's milk of language, water with a whitish stain".

III

The damned disputations flow infinitely
I am a living man, furry, with full armoury

— I made my choice.

The beetle and the piano

Upon finding itself in the unfamiliar environment of lathed wood
and strung wire
(the piano)
the beetle forgot its training
and panicked.

- I must emphasise that we are not talking about a novice beetle,
but a stag
with experience of gardens, small forests
and certain enclosed spaces -

The error had been in the association of the instrument's gloss
paint with a larger beetle

Despite that, no sexual motive was imputed

It is possible it had mistaken it for a larger cousin

Nevertheless, its mistake was compounded and the concert fierce.
It jumped desperately from clef to clef, dodging the keys, heroic

Finally, the third movement tired it.
I watched the struggle between felt pads

One wing case loose. His legs were kicking high, ballet-like

Then a bass note, forte

Hamlet, reviewed

Rzelenko Konstantin was the Prince of Denmark
his peace a parried extinction, clutching at a friend's head and
whirling a sword stick into the line of the sea
the revolution of circles
two faces forerunning the hot foam
the bones burnished by the gentle rub of sand.

He ached. This choice between
consumptives and skulls.
Absurd. In this hissing hinterland
death by water.

First edition

(a hundred years ago)
Maria wrote "I love you"
in the book that she was reading
today I read it and wrote back
that I returned the feeling

A prayer before retiring

O lord keep the white border of a murmuring world
the boundary of the day's brightness
and keep from us the teeth of phosphored things
that dwell in the deepening oceans.

Deep. Dark. Beyond the grae of midday shining
the mirror waters. Black and obstinate as volcanic glass
the failed creation of a hungry god
nightmares slicked against a wall of night

Deliver us from teeth of phosphor
the ribboned, snaked eyes
the whorled faces of fingers
O lord.

Bitterness

Three flavours on my palate met:
sweet, salt, sour.

Three flavours now, which I savour yet:
sweet, salt, sour.

For fruit is good, and fruit is sweet,
but fruit alone is not good to eat:
sweet, salt, sour.

And salt preserves, and salt makes us strong
but who can sup tears all night long?
Sweet, salt, sour.

Sour is a sharp which cuts with each sip
sour as the lemon which bloodies the lip:
sweet, salt, sour.

Sweet in the day, and salt in the night,
and sour like a scent which lingers in flight
(but will not stay)
away with your sweet, salt, sour.

Box

Glittered bric-a-brac piled in miser's loads
the weight and ornament of cored survival
tire and check and ruin heaped and tallied
the shipwreck of ivory, the faultline of silver.

A pander of rectangled love, and inside the squared sides snug:
hope.

Companion

To pass like the yeast in fine bread:
no one comments on it, nor discerns it
yet the bread rises.

To stay only for the instant of tasting
like the savour of wine
to remain as warmth and fire
as a cup of joy.

To last as nourishment lasts
to endure, as fragrance does
to live in simple things
until the evening comes.

Faith

The two: the earth of angry mercies and
an orient of serene light.

They nestle under the heart, framed by a halo of spines.
Sharper than saints
cleaner than sugar

If I could call them from my breast
break the ribs, the white seed beneath the bone
then, at the soul's harvest
I would give to anyone who asked

The Wilton Diptych

Who rules here?
The startled Christ who clutches for the gift?
No, here the donor is divine:
a banner of glorious angels bear his sign
and a saintly line of kings commend him.
In kneeling he is higher than the seraphs:
that ginger boy, noble face profiled
his full portrayal would surpass the sun.

Bolingbroke's white hart
is a sneer in blue and gold, precociously done.
Perhaps providence smiled, and graced it
with a threadbare immortality.
For Wilton's craft endured
the crushing hands of men
who more than art, loved God.

Rood

Hail, glory-tree, ship wood of paradise
who carried the All-King to his high seat
life returned to life, soul fled
on cold paths to seek the places behind the stars.

Lo, wrath-ward. Your branches bore the weight
of judgement. And this noble strain budded forth
a fragrant mercy on whose stems
Hell's strength broke in cymbals
of rotten and discordant steel.

Hail, fruit of Eden. Thy roots speak
of eternal things. From the blooded soil
a fresh and ageless beauty ventures forth,
unbinding the ancient serpent's interdict
to mark mankind for endless days
with deathlessness and words of gold.

Saffron

In memory of Christine, anchoress of Shere

In this village we brick the women up
but I mixed the mortar with too much lime
time and your fingernails
worked out the seam.

I cut stone, but you were the true mistress of
Surrey's bony earth. In the navel of the church
your song soaked the pillars
a tone of crushed oil, more penetrating than myrrh
anointed the air.

Like pressed seeds and stamens
are women in the house of God
like lilac and burnt sap
their hot sighs ascend.

In this quiet garden, in this time of singed music
hemmed in by glass and Zion's songs
I would have you grow in joy.
O my saffron. My limeflower.

Professor

I sit in the democracy of the dying
spindle-limbed, with a bulging belly like a tulip bulb
germinating the lines of books:
swords with golden hilts
toothed axes and singing spears
skeletal buttercups on the fields of war.

A job to think on these things, but as the legions say;
pretium victoriae.

Brutus

It was an adam blade
a gladius, plain, pitted
a killing tool.

In the brillante weirdness of a wound
the flesh suddenly gapped and unstoppered
came a poison of silences, poised
balanced on the flawed sculpture of your face
eyes wide, wider than the wind
and deep within, that ravenous expanse.

Auxiliary

Lucius, to his Emperor, greetings.

August lord, forgive this rough soldier's scrawl
I write well but my hand was cleaved in
three Spanish campaigns. All my blue scars shine
like gemstones: the underscore of my eyes.
I bought the rank of Palatine with cuts
and my courage was repaid in pure salt.

The Legion has been here twenty winters.
The chestnut fields are always fat with rain.
It pours on Apollo's feasts, which makes the
priest squirm. The barbarians steal our grain
and sell the lads barley wine and slave-girls.
Sarmatians. Worse than Egypt's petty crooks.

Divine master, send relief. Scythians
hem us in like sheep and the time grows close
when our own strength will not suffice to stand.
I ask, and only that — for now we have
endured heat flies and ambushes at night.
We are your own, and wait for your command.

Temptation

Anthony: you went into the desert, and made it your friend
the wild beasts were afraid of you:
an angel with six hundred wings
guarded your sleep.

But the enemy is sleepless, and came
in the carmine split of thoughts
the neon worm-electric
darting coronas behind the eyelids.

Women- nubile, succulent
more beautiful than badgers, classier than fitted kitchens
eyes bright like polished taps.

And possessions
a fine steam engine, a collection of beer widgets
frog eye marbles
scores of them

The thrill of command
the freeze of briny emotion
cold orders presented with
the face of a preserved fish

Ha. You shooed away the Devil
with a chuckle, that turned into a hoot
and then a belly laugh.
That is simplicity without flourish. Holiness.

Toledo

I

Those sly, darting looks
have pierced the skin
those glances, like lances
have brought blood to my cheeks.

II

I, the lioness. I have scorned kings
no cur will be my mate
your little bark is wasted
when I am deaf to the roaring prides.

III

The Prophet, blessings on him, said
"Come to your women
not like beasts,
but forge the link."

IV

What is the link?

V

The kiss.

VI

It would be like hot solder, like metal to my mouth.

VII

Not so. Courtesy is like the ready grape
musk and ruddy wine
mingled, dashed with clean water
for parched throats.

VIII

The day burns.

IX

Drink. And then you shall see hazelnuts smoking
listen to red music
ride horses from the stud farms of Spain
the cloistered gardens will seem to you
like new palaces.

Stallion

Suffer not lady, to take your eyes from me
I sought the beauty of your face for hungry years
that purchased honour for my prince.
Strange lands became like home on my travelling
I rode through the thirsty lands
and walked through the wet lands
my passage was through the dry lands
what was home has passed into unknowing.

My head was turned towards the evening
the breath of the Daystar still buried in my cheeks
it was cut from light and the dreams of seraphim
that royal face behind the sun.

The sun shall pass it to the west
the moon will raise it to the east
the rain has begun
my imagination kneels before those drenched lineaments
the cut of the nose, the fall of the eyelids.

Couched, supine lances, stars at my heels
the skies bright burning, bright monstrance
the storm's silence before that countenance.

Galliard

I

Satin, slipper chapel
a walled Walsingham
where in the garden unseen
steals the fairy queen.

In that paradise of suns
courtesy is held
all unbred barbarity
expelled.

So in Greek minuet
I string my steps to sing
and in hoplite harmony
spring.

II

My hands hold the flowing grape
the symbol and the sign
steel gloves from my fingers press
wine.

Beneath that spray the earth is glad
with autumn's setting spice
each dressed leaf a knightly shield,
device.

Here the torrent Cedron flowed

and here I drink the lees
a vintage hot with seven sips
Gethsemane's.

III

Let my words be witnessed
by the sky of Roman rays
while the earth with ruby leaf
its strongest shield displays
the time between the soil and light
is mine to give away
and I am yours
in hand and foot
whilst the sun sustains the day.

Asp

The gathering of strangers
I became a stranger to myself
in this swarm of Egyptians.

You had a nose like notes, falling to
circled shoes of small black, round like quavers
your voice like the Nile in summer
a drowsy copper melody
hissing to a far sea

You sing in the peril of my touch
I sway in the danger of your song
the dance goes on, but the music is only for a time
the pierce of my mouth, the sigh of your song:
we are both sleep for each other.

Canticle

The gusts of Persia will glow upon the glades
and cause the rain to vanish. In the shade
of many trees I will abide, and dream, and whisper
and love.

I have yet to tell you the most beautiful things
Wait! And do not be dismayed
my word is coming and will not be delayed.

Rossetti's changeling

Sleep, little Baby, sleep.

Holy Innocents

It is a kindling thought, with my own features,
the smaller imprint of my face,
small but familiar
cribbed in smooth sheets.

For forty years I thought my prince would come,
and so, I played coy games, delights half devoured
sweet fruits of the goblin markets.
I danced the dribbled juice in Italian steps,
trotted the time away while round
the fairy rings the seasons reeled and the
earth was dry with blood.

No long looks for me, not now, no
calling in the markets, no caw of goblin men,
no leering dwarfs, no prince no prince and now
my mind is strafing the sky like pikes
the half night of the south, the bisected day
and all the light impaled

I pick up the pillow, embroided with richest threads
of steel
and wrap my fairy child
with naked sheets of iron.

Priestess

Delphi. Brimming with broth and circumcision
the bubbling and the nick of knives
little cauldrons of chaos, hubbub of bubbles —
but the oracle stays serene,
her nights dark. Pure. Perfumed.
Apollo's Pearl. With her cuts she brings forth
adroit mysteries.

Composition

With folds of final cream, you trimmed the black almonds with
heron glances.
Watching. The ink pleats chased the bronze buttons,
buttons and bottled beer.

In these Roman robes
sandals beaded with the dust of home
in the shimmer of London's wet streets
you walked with steps of silk
gave Martin's cloak away:
for charity is colour
and love the spray of vivid paint.

The summer country

There is a felt to light, a breath to noise
a wrinkled nose to touch
there impressions which a finger leaves
gossamer, dust-like indentations
the meteors of sunlight bursting on the skin

Tender touch which bids the laurel flower
the bee his harvest to commence and
all this labour recompense.

Noon

When I think of it
I walk outside myself
and summer lengthens the legs of girls
while dark clouds of ants shade the ground
a freckled breeze whirls the pollen

We talked about Issa and his affinity for cats
in roundabout way
all art is about the innocence of cats
and small children playing.

Katana

Steel is born in pain, tears of red glass crying
the heron sings against the sky
a birth, a dying.

> But swords are born in skill and joy
> in sparks weaned strong
> from the forge, furnace tested
> then in the waters rested.

Swords are steel, and skill is found
in the heavy hammerhand, in the sound
strike of craft.

> There is also silence in the steel,
> before the hammers on the anvil peal
> silence sounds as the lightning soars
> heaven is hushed before the thunder roars.

Enough. This blade alights
on the edgeland of Cold Nights
quenched in necks, its accolade.

> Cold is the grip that grasps the rayskin hilt
> that unfeeling cuts.
> Better the blow that with honour lands
> held in Warm Hands.

Trial by water — blue your blade
in the whirling shaded stream
we shall see whose truth cuts clean.

You are the master only of the blade
which slices when you should have stayed
the killing stroke. With hate your art was made
and scarlet dyes the jade waters.

Aphex

The sailor had a mizzenmast face
his home the underside of the firmament
he had mixed his dreams with brine
in Japan, he hired two whores
but his strength was like seawater
and the first had drowned him

Thereafter, his lips had
the crackle of crushed butterflies
the grind at the end of innocence
every smile was the wetness of exposed bone
his glances dripped like seaweed
lay wet and fly-blown.

Outremer

Was it curiosity or irritation
that inclined the elegance of your frame
and spirited a perfect pirouette
you became a dancer for God
with splayed feet.

Perhaps it was the call of heels
the double tap of turned leather
the eloquence of silk and tended skinscapes
the tincture of chrysanthemums
and irises like burnt cloud.

Ah, Jaufre. It was pity
the right brow cocked like a gun
at the dull slap of flesh on stone
at the crumbling of thigh and calf
at that fatal moment
you looked for your lady's shadow.

Despair comes.
Hysteria and wine
will scatter your limbs
Prince of Blaise.

Homecoming

Scarborough's dark brown sea
rocking with memories
like ranks of chestnuts falling
the smell of crushed herbs

I have trod this Northern style
where freighted ice is beneath the smile
and beg you: no wet white water,
from brittle loves give respite,
let me rest awhile.

Here is your cambric shirt
seamless and shining
bees' work in wax, no needle
has ever grazed it.
I pooled my tears, and with that well-water
washed it.

From where they martyred Magnus
in arctic sails I caught the dancing wind
and found a place thick with ice and
only the sea beneath. So with
a breaking, beaked ship
I ploughed an acre of land
between the salt water and the sea strand
while the whales roared.

So dear I have finished my task
parsley, sage, rosemary and thyme
I come to you, your hand for to ask

Émigré

He stewed his thoughts like tea leaves,
fingering the samovar
the metal warm in lattices.
The notches too thin for fingers.
It might have been an heirloom
(but rust has no heritage).

The walls bent with icons —
faces of gold and tin plate,
white glasses of vodka, books
and the borrowed illumination
deftly stolen from an unheard Russian dawn.

Hetman

trans. from the Polish.

Let Roman might outstrip our armies
India exceed us with its gold-giving rivers
more precious than those shining waters
are rich Polish liberties.

She freely chose her king and lord:
Sigismund. His crown fixed
her borders deep in heaven's circuit
to the far north.

In her sacred cause, justice stands and
virtue flowers. Thanks to you, oh God
that wrath and hateful jealousy
unmoving lie.

Whilst the Oder sea-bound streams
Zamoyski's name endures, the Persians
and black Mauritians know it.
Africa hears it.

Neva's Queen

On the anniversary of the death of Anna Akhmatova

In my curled thoughts, I returned to my Russian
mourning the husband of her half-loves
cutting thick swathes of violets into vases
suddenly tearful
at the sound of his patronym.

The third of May

What potent blood hath modest May;
what fiery force the earth renews.

May-Day

May is our wedding garment
where the bridegroom's party wreathes
us with burning words and nature
calls the fertile soil to stand
in shapes of green and gold.

Here we have breathed bread and salt
and in tall forests sung the branches higher
whilst fires of friendship warmed the glowing night.

May, when we walk in the cadence of sad courts.
With tears like long moustaches we toast
Warsaw's palaces, burning like bushels.
We eat exile's bread
dodge Babcia's stoneware pots
and remember home's bright hills.

God, we have worn our cavalry shoes
and *kontusze* down in dances.
Here we have laughed, bled,
sped letters in princely hands of love
walked with cross, crescent, star
ages have spun: now we live, we are
dressed with seals of joy.

O my people, we are all garments
for each other

A Silesian coalman's return

From the white-out of shaken clouds
comes the enameled frost. Each flake a brush to paint out the
signature of sex.
That is the difference that snow makes:
we look the same, we dress the same. (You can still spot the men —
a head taller in their hats.)

The white-out of a slender sky
painting with enamel, brushing away
the lines between male and female,
dusting the borders of sex with frost.
This is the difference that snow makes:
we dress the same and height
becomes an unsure measure to tell us apart.

The mine's forgotten now. And this place of small difference?
This clean, cold world? Nah.
Give me my pillowed wife
a bath studded with suds
and slippers warming by the radiator.

Poznan

Inside high portals rising
the headless lions roar
their paws impatient
the chipped brass concealing
a reversion of dust to dust
muting my chimed words to stillness.

Stone and tomb. The slow smell of soil cut with incense.
The altar bathes the martyrs' bones in wine.
Around, my forefathers, with their wood and clay faces
arms in stucco and pierced metal: horsemen hunting eagles.

This thin place, where a cross of stone has chiselled
(for ten centuries)
the lower floor of heaven.

Horae mortis

Sliced moonlight, cut like cheesecake
the half-circle of white glare: a moon of cats
the night majestic in silence
when above the terror of mouse-waters
death came with a banana.

Death, death is a little lavender boy
with gold dimples
twinkling, dustlike indentations
he smiles prettily at me.

His the wet, embalming hour
amber poured round my mouth
a snarf of orange and watery breath
like an invalid sodden with shoelaces
at last I come to the knot of things.

I see that life is piggybacks and stretched glass
if the king of the universe is my friend
magpies
midnight
miracles
will wait for my drip of jewels.

Power

Its strength seductive
that fatal, charged chair:
a perilous seat, for around the throne the thunder howls.

Nevertheless, the current calls
as much as any woman, and I appreciate
the enjoyable thrum of electric legs
the rictus pleasures of wire and static:
a face juddering to the faint hiss of smoke.

Torrent

The last waters are not cruel to them.
They shall not fear the noonday sun,
nor bullets, nor bitter solitude, nor plagues.
These have been washed away.

All things are forgotten there, that deserve it
and they alone are held in everlasting remembrance — like stone
pillars sunk beneath the waves.

Time will carry me there, by long leagues and crossed waters, until
the second immersion:
then I will bind the strong one
and have power to walk on snakes and scorpions.

Until then, Lethe, river of forgetfulness,
help me forget my own death.

The guard of flowers

Vanilla's silken scent, seductive, slippery to touch
it draped the room like oriental fabric.

Kapayati traced the theorem with
his face frantic
his brow dewed
a blubbery press of jowls
(the cut flowers do not exist for him)

Equation: technocrat
polysexual
unbound by family
untouched by dogma
unlettered by past thoughts

He (it is always he) is creating
the new man
of liquid flesh,
rippling
un dulating on the blue pages
like the throat-sack of some tropical bird

And will he triumph?
You know, you have always known
that flowers cannot save us

Candlemas

These cells of light, glowing with
the fat of flowers,
the entrails of summer:
it rises to a rhyme, the hum of fire
the laughing buds of radiant heat.

Oh, attend those burning prayers of bees
the censered sound of poured honey
a guttering, dribbled benediction,
and in the temple all the insects cry:

Glory.

Cog

A flat disk, metal, notched —
in motion.

(Let us observe it).

Principio. The cog moves with the other cogs, apart from them
there is no movement.

So you concede interdependence.

Secundum. There is a finite number of cogs. Helium and hydrogen
are the natural elements, all heavier forms are forged in the corona
of a star.

(Pharoah's Proof. Numbers are fixed — the first Shoah was almost
a success.)

So you concede particularity.

Tertio. The visual omits the thermal. The cog has friction,
pressure, it shatters, melts. One day a cog could flare and, igneous,
bring the superheat of suns
into the belly of the machine.

So you must take chaos into account.

In sum: no cog, then — rather, Sir, no, Lord Cogito!
Each common cog bearing
this precious load of freedom
in daily iteration

You are an oriflamme of steel, the singed blood of comets
at the appointed time

— your heat will blister faces

The Decollation of St James

I was born under the rumble of heaven.
My name uncurling like lightning on a velvet sky: jakobbarzebidi.
My mother's choice. It was commented upon.

I was unsure of birth.
There is never certainty. You can always ask another question
tear another thought, have the mind betray you once again.
Birth was unsure — shall I be unsteady in death?

(Oh, if I have failed then
I hope there is a reason for my failure)

Sometimes we are wounds within wounds.
The abrasions concealing gashes within
then even tenderness is unbearable
I have always held the courage in my eyes — eyes like rifles

No skittishness now,
for powderfood:
I will testify with my flesh
with the pale fire of faith.

I am the last bang in this gunpowder square

Palms

*A marvellous and worthy work, the delight of the whole earth,
beautiful and more lovely than the beautiful. - George Sphrantzes*

So come away with me
on the highest and the hardest paths.
We'll break bread on the road of falcons, in the eyrie of elect spirits.
Gabriel will meet us,
and hit me on the head with peacock feathers.
Michael will develop a fascination with his feet, and scabbard his sword away.
Raphael will light us crisp cigarettes on his halo.

You are allowed to listen to that word
Your love calling out to the Other
dazzling my wounds
the palms smiling in your hands

Notes

The Clotheshorse, the ghost of London – London has clothes lying around the streets, in odd combinations and places, if you look carefully enough. This is a riff based on that observation.

The words we write – this is a reference to the styles of troubadour poetry, specifically to a dispute as to whether *trobar leu* (light poetry) or *trobar clus* (difficult or closed poetry) was better.

Katana – a reimagining of an old Japanese story about two smiths, one who forged with hate, one otherwise.

Outremer – about Jaufre Rudel, a French prince, who went, so the story goes, on Crusade for love and who died in Tripoli.

Horae mortis – a fever dream when dying.

Cog – a nod here to Zbigniew Herbert and his character of Mr Cogito.

Gabriel Olearnik was born to a Polish family but raised and educated in London. His education has included medieval literature and history, the law, and time in both Warsaw and Rome. His work has been published extensively in the United States and his previous volume of poetry, *Amor de Lonh*, received favourable critical review internationally. *Gunpowder Square* is his second collection.

Three Shoes Books is the Poetry Press of the Cheltenham Poetry Festival

www.ingramcontent.com/pod-product-compliance
Lightning Source LLC
Chambersburg PA
CBHW061251040426
42444CB00010B/2353